Fashions IN THE GROOVE

'60s & '70s

JOE POLTORAK

Schiffer Publishing Ltd

4880 Lower Valley Rd. Atglen, PA 19310 USA

Dedication

To Barb, my son Jesse, and my parents.

Copyright © 1998 by Joe Poltorak
Library of Congress Catalog Card Number: 98-85073

Designed by Bonnie M. Hensley
Typeset in Geometric 231 BT/Times New Roman

ISBN: 0-7643-0620-0
Printed in China
1 2 3 4

Published by Schiffer Publishing Ltd.
4880 Lower Valley Road
Atglen, PA 19310
Phone: (610) 593-1777; Fax: (610) 593-2002
E-mail: Schifferbk@aol.com

In Europe Schiffer books are distributed by
Bushwood Books
6 Marksbury Avenue Kew Gardens
Surrey TW9 4JF England
Phone: 44 (0) 181 392-8585; Fax: 44 (0) 181 392-9876
E-mail: Bushwd@aol.com

Please write for a free catalog.
This book may be purchased from the publisher.
Please include $3.95 for shipping.
Please try your bookstore first.
We are interested in hearing from authors
with book ideas on related subjects.

Contents

DISCARDED

*F*oreword by Patricia McLaughlin 5

*A*cknowledgments 7

*I*ntroduction 9

*C*hapter One: Men's Shirts and Sweaters 11
    Italian Knits, Sweaters, and Banlons 11
    Shirt-Jacs, Button Downs, Nehru, and Tab Collars 26
    Polyester Shirts 30
    T-shirts 43

*C*hapter Two: Cool Pants 55
    Straight-leg Pants 55
    Wild Things 62
    Hip Huggers and Elephant Bells 76
    Baggies and Disco Flares 80

*C*hapter Three: Skimpy Swimwear and Surfin' Shorts 87

*C*hapter Four: Dresses 101
    Patio Prints 101
    Goin' Out Dresses 106

*C*hapter Five: All The Rest 111
    Skirts, Shorts, and Jeans 111
    Stretchy Tops 118
    T-shirts and Tanks 139
    Halters, Tube Tops, and Sizzling Hot Pants 151

Foreword

Travels with Joe

By Patricia McLaughlin

Joe Poltorak wanders the small towns of Middle America, raising brand new clothes from the dead.

If you're the sort of person who likes driving back roads and poking around in little old dusty country stores and listening to the life stories of people you'll probably never see again and digging through attics and basements nobody has cleaned out in years and eating blue plate specials in small-town diners, you'll be jealous of Joe Poltorak.

That's his job.

It started in 1976, on a trip to London, when he took along a suitcase full of American bowling shirts and sold enough at the Portabello Road flea market to cover his plane fare. Dealers would come up to him and ask, could he get more? He could and he did, and he's still doing it.

Now he's more likely to be looking for a gross of Maverick bellbottom jeans that some little dry goods store in Mississippi over ordered in 1969 and got stuck with and still has packed away in the stockroom. "When bellbottoms died, they died fast," he says, "and people got stuck with some pretty big inventories."

Or all the hot pants from a dress shop in central Pennsylvania that got stored in somebody's garage back in 1971 when the shop burned. Or a thousand pairs of sensible ladies oxfords that some shoe store owner figured he could sell any amount of in 1960, because they were what old ladies had been wearing practically forever—but, by 1967, nobody wanted them anymore because they looked to old-ladyish, and even old ladies wanted to join the Pepsi Generation.

His specialty is the fashion trends of the 1960s and 1970s, styles that reflect the heady days when all sorts of things that would shape American fashion and popular culture through the end of the millennium were being born: the youth culture, the Sexual Revolution, surfing, Black Power, psychedelia and the drug culture, do your own thing, tail fins and television, Op and Pop, and a couple dozen more.

Poltorak is an unaccredited archaeologist of the recent past. He digs up things that remind us of who we used to be just a few decades ago—and, because those things disappeared so fast, we're surprised to see them again. He goes for things that are iconic, styles that evoke the hope and innocence and optimism and bittersweet certainties that vanished with the era. Striped T-shirts like those that Wally and the Beaver and the Brady Bunch wore. Wallpaper print shirts from the Flower Power era, with collar points as long and droopy as a hound dog's ears. Miniskirts you knew were the right length if your fingertips brushed the hem. Dresses with labels that said "PermaPress" and "Drip Dry." Cool

Italian knit shirts with graphic patterns—*tres moderne*—and sprinkles of glitter. Pint-size cowboy boots. Cotton socks still marked "49 cents." Dresses with hang tags that show a smiling mom ironing in high heels. Jeans meant for—as the hang tag says—"the in group that is really with it."

Poltorak himself can hardly believe people still have this stuff, but they do. Most of his suppliers, he says, are still in business more out of inertia than anything else. Mostly, they own their buildings, so they aren't paying rent, and they don't want to retire, because then where would they go every morning? They'll tell him how they used to have seven salesmen and two tailors; now it's just them. And out back in the shed, or up in the attic, or down in the cellar is all the stuff they couldn't sell forty and thirty and twenty years ago and thought they'd never get rid of. He buys it for cash, and sometimes they'll tell him about a place in the next town, or somebody who bought out the stock of an old general store a couple of years ago and probably still has it.

That's when he's lucky. When he isn't, they say, "Gosh, you should've been here last year, before we paid 'em to cart all that stuff in the barn down to the dump, truckloads of it." It's especially painful when he knew about the place last year, but took too long to get to it.

He finds all sorts of things. One time he found a brown paper bag full of money that the shop owner had forgotten about and was delighted to rediscover. Another time, he spent the day pitching stacks of sequined dresses out the second-story window of a row house because the place was so jammed with the stock of a one-time dress shop it would've taken forever to get them down the stairs and through the choked hallways.

Poltorak calls the stuff he buys dead stock. It's old, but it's brand new, never-been-worn, still has the tags on it.

Some of it goes to dealers in Japan and Europe who'll pay astronomical prices for rare vintage blue jeans or authentic cowboy shirts or pristine 1960s bellbottoms. What they're buying along with the clothes, he says, is a little piece of the American Dream, an authentic artifact of the gorgeous American pop culture that fascinates them—and no wonder, to hear Poltorak tell it; "We have Harley-Davidson and Elvis and Cadillacs and movie stars! It's our culture: Cowboys! Singing cowboys!"

Some of the stuff he finds stays here, and it means something a little bit different to the people who buy it here. It connects them to a past they've read about, or heard about, or vaguely remember from when they were little kids, a past that may seem cooler or quainter or more lovable because it's beyond reach and they don't remember the bad parts.

Some of his best stuff is in this book, and just looking at it takes you back to its time in a way that reading history books can't. Check out these bellbottoms, itsy-bitsy bikinis, miniskirts, and splashy polyester prints and you get an immediate shot of the flavor, the attitude and energy, the taste (and lack thereof) of another time.

Acknowledgements

I want to thank the following friends for sharing their thoughts and collections. Without their generosity and support this book would never have been written. They will be happy to know that their trip to the sixties and seventies is now over and they can adjust their TV sets and return to the nineties.

Jesse and Wanda: For their many hours of patience and support through this project.

Gail and Bill Whitman: For helping me remember what we wore and when.

Kelly Whalen (Wear It Again Sam, 4237 Main Street Philadelphia, PA 19127 (215-487-0525)): for introducing me to Peter and Doug.

Julie Berry: Thanks for her tireless energy in selecting the clothes, coordinating the photo shoot, and all those pep talks.

Patsy McLaughlin: Thanks for getting my thoughts out of my head and onto paper.

Kate Dolan

Elizabeth Hine

Dennie Dolan: So glad you hung onto those shirts for so long.

Toshi Tanahashi

Suheil Cabrera: Thanks for making the clothes look so good.

Tina , Bruce, Peter, Doug and all staff of Schiffer Publishing: for making this project go so smoothly.

Lastly, but most especially, Barbara Schuette: Not only for her love, but also for the continuous effort she gave to every single aspect of this book. She gets a tiara, two tickets to the circus, and a pony.

Introduction

I can remember the first thrift store I was ever in. My mother took me there in 1956 when I was 8 years old. It was actually two narrow stores connected by a large doorway and a short ramp. Bare wooden floors creaked as you walked, adding to the mystery. The toys were in the room to the right and that's where I disappeared to. There were boxes and boxes of them. Dozens of bicycles, scooters, pedal cars, and rocking horses lined the floor of one entire wall. My mother spent her time among the coats and dresses, and for that one brief hour I had more toys than my cousin, Ziggy.

I wish I had a time machine.

Fast forward forty years and I find myself once again in old stores with creaking floors. This time in the back rooms and basements of shops that were in business before World War II, before the Great Depression, before airplanes. And while I search the shelves for the forgotten bell bottoms and other stragglers, the shop's owner invariably gives me the entire history of the store, the town, and any other advice he or she feels is necessary to tell.

To say that I love my work would be an understatement.

Chapter One

Men's Shirts and Sweaters

Italian Knits, Sweaters and Banlons

In the early '60s you needed to have had a job, or a brother who did, in order to afford Italian knits. If you wore them, you probably listened to doo-wop music, had a friend with a convertible, and used Brylcream. You never lent these shirts out, not even to your best buddy (it was always "at the cleaners"). And if you wore your most expensive one on a date, it meant you really liked her. The idea was to look as much like Frankie Avalon, Duane Eddy, or Fabian, as you could.

Italian knit shirt with three-tone coloring and vertical pleats. 1960s. Wool. ($65-85)

Italian knit shirts. Covered buttons and vertically graduated color design. Wool. 1960s. ($65-85)

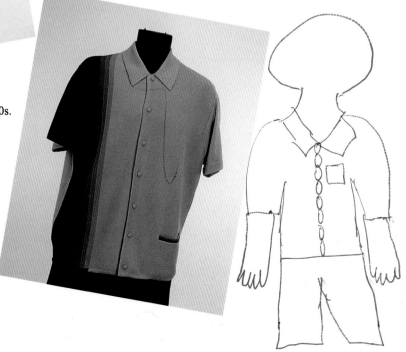

Italian knit shirt. Short-sleeve pullover. Wool/
cotton blend. 1960s. ($60-75)

Italian knit shirts. Pullover with
ornamental buckle at waist. Wide
track vertical stripes. Wool. 1960s.
($75-95)

Italian knit shirts. Mohair front with cable knit panels. Wool. 1960s. ($50-60)

Italian knit shirt with full zip front. Multi-color vertical stripe pattern. Wool. 1970s. ($65-70)

Italian knit shirts with
mock turtle inset.
Acrylic. Late 1960s.
($35-45)

Italian knit shirts with
mock cross over vest.
1960s. Wool. ($65-85)

Pullover with mock turtle. Three-tone coloring. Acrylic. 1960s. ($30-40)

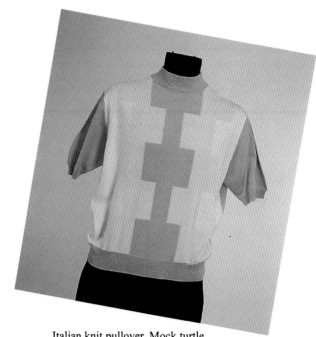

Italian knit pullover. Mock turtle. Wool. 1960s. ($40-50)

Shirt with mock turtle. Royal blue with cable edged insert. Buttons at waistband. Nylon. Late 1960s to early 1970s. ($35-45)

Shirts with crew necks and striped front insert. Black, gold, royal blue. Acetate. Late 1960s to early 1970s. ($28-35)

Let It All Hang Out

Banlon® shirts by Campus®
with single breast pocket.
Long sleeves. Olive, Gold.
Nylon. 1970s. ($25-30)

Banlon® pullover shirts by Cam-
pus®. Long sleeves and covered
buttons. Nylon. Late 1960s to early
1970s. ($35-45)

Italian-made shirts. Short sleeves with
covered buttons. Pink/Purple. Acetate.
1960s. ($40-48)

Pullover shirt with
mock turtle neck.
Acrylic. Late 1960s
to early 1970s.
($25-30)

16

Italian knit sweater. Beautiful diamond
knit pattern. 100 percent wool. 1960s.
($65-85)

Italian knit sweater. Classic color
combinations for this period. 100
percent wool. 1960s. ($65-85)

17

Italian knit sweater. Front button cardigan with collar. Yellow with gold honeycomb pattern on front. 100 percent wool. 1960s. ($60-75)

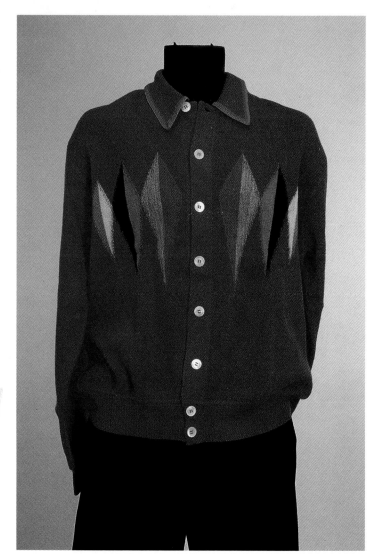

Italian knit sweater. Rare color combinations. 100 percent wool. 1960s. ($65-85)

Italian knit sweater with front belt between contrasting cable panels. 100 percent wool. 1960s. ($65-85)

Italian knit shirt with a double breasted look. Plum and baby blue. Wool. 1960s. ($50-60)

18

Boldly colored Italian shirt
with covered buttons.
Acetate. Late 1960s to early
1970s. ($45-60)

Italian knit shirt with
front zip closure.
Acetate. 1970s. ($45-55)

Checkerboard pattern Banlon®
shirt. Nylon. Late 1960s to early
1970s. ($55-65)

Italian knit shirt with satin
covered buttons and front
pleats. Wool. Late 1960s.
($50-65)

Bulky knit cardigans with front
panel stripes. Acrylic. 1960s.
($28-36)

Two-tone ribbed turtleneck
sweaters. Acrylic. 1970s.
($35-45)

Cardigan style sweater with
the new "suede look". Brown.
Acrylic. 1960s. ($40)

Bulky knit crew neck
sweater. Acrylic. 1970s.
($25-35)

McGregor® pullover sweater. Gold "shag." Mohair and wool. 1960s. ($35-45)

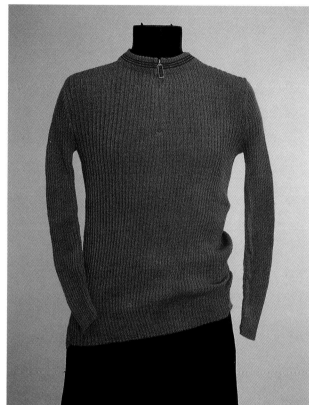

Men's long sleeve sweater. Front half zip. Salmon color. Polyester knit. 1970s. ($25-35)

Ribbed knit sweater with front half zip. Acrylic. 1970s. ($25-35)

Henley style sweater with long sleeves by Campus®. 100 percent virgin orlon acrylic. 1970s. ($25-35)

Fruit of the Loom® striped
pullover sweaters. Variegated rib
with collar and half zip. Acrylic.
1970s. ($28-36)

Multi color sweater with collar
and single button at V-neck.
1970s. Acrylic. ($25-35)

Pullover sweater with collar and single
button at V-neck. Bulky knit. 1970s.
Acrylic. ($25-35)

V-neck sweater with varsity
striping. Pullover. 1970s.
Acrylic. ($28-36)

Shirt-Jacs, Button Downs, Nehru, and Tab Collars

Men's shirts of the '60s covered a wide range of looks, from Elvis to the British Invasion. In the early '60s men knew what they were supposed to wear to be cool. By the end of the '60s there were more options. What you wore was determined mostly by your musical taste and political ideology.

Arrow® shirt-Jac. Gray and beige vertical stripes. Slash breast pocket with buttons at waist. Rayon/acetate/silk blend. 1960s. ($35-45)

Shirt-Jacs. Two tone with hidden breast pockets. 100 percent cotton. 1960s. ($35-45)

Knit shirt jacs with pockets at waist. 100 percent cotton. 1960s. ($35-45)

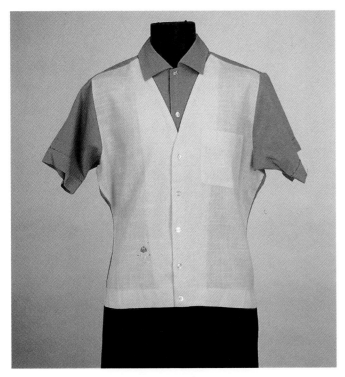

Puritan® shirt jac with mock vest front.
Rayon/cotton blend. 1960s. ($35-45)

Model wearing '60s shirt jac with hot pants.

27

Cotton shirts with button-down collars and mini polka dots. 1960s. ($20-30)

Cotton shirts with button-down collar with large polka dots. 1960s. ($20-30)

Town Tropic® Ivy League shirts with button-down collar. Paisley prints. 100 percent cotton. 1960s. ($20-30)

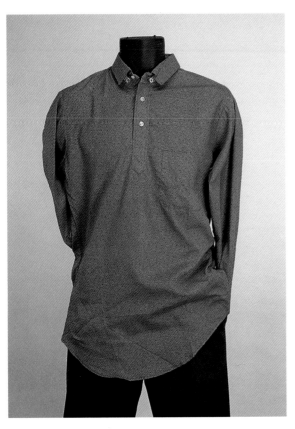

Tab collar shirt. Sedgefield by Blue Bell®. 1960s. 100 percent cotton. ($25-35)

Campus® formal shirt. Brocade with covered buttons. Late 1960s. Cotton/ acetate. ($45-50)

BVD® Nehru style shirt. Paisley print. 100 percent cotton. Late 1960s. ($36-45)

Polyester Shirts

Polyester print shirts don't need me to speak for them. They speak loudly enough on their own. They were best worn nice and tight with the top three buttons undone and a large gold medallion decorating your chest. If you liked them at all, you liked them a lot and probably owned quite a few. Like the Hawaiian shirts of the '40s, these gems are becoming increasingly popular among collectors for their boldly printed colors and patterns.

Impressionistic print shirt. 1970s. Polyester. ($20-30)

"Expressions" by Campus® shirts with geometric prints. Late 1960s to early1970s. Polyester/cotton. ($20-30)

polyester

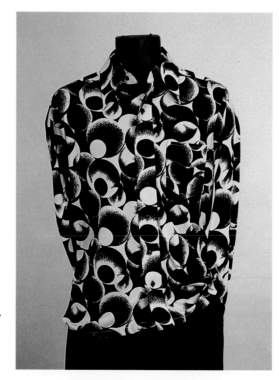

Shirt with high contrast geometric pattern. 1970s. Nylon. ($20-30)

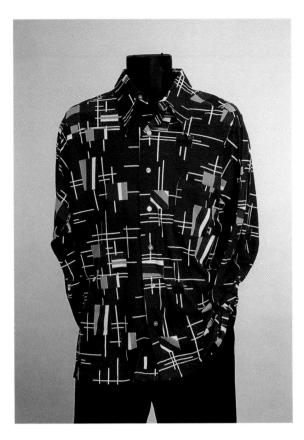

McGregor ® brand
shirt. Geometric print.
1970s. Polyester.
($20-30)

Polka dot shirts. 1970s. Polyester.
($20-30)

Zigzag-patterned shirts. Late
1960s to early1970s.
Polyester. ($20-30)

Print shirts. Polyester/cotton. Late
1960s to early 1970s. ($16-24)

Shirt with multi color vertical stripes. Polyester. Late 1960s to early 1970s. ($20-30)

Bold patchwork print shirts with white collars. Late 1960s to early 1970s. Polyester/cotton. ($16-24)

Maverick® brand shirt. Circular geometric print. Late 1960s to early 1970s. Polyester/cotton . ($16-24)

Maverick® brand shirt. Red geometric print. Polyester/cotton. Late 1960s to early 1970s. ($16-24)

Shirt and tie coordinates.
1970s. Polyester/cotton.
($16-24)

Tuxedo shirts.
Tapered body and
balloon sleeves.
1970s. Polyester/
cotton. ($20-25)

Maverick® brand print
shirts with solid yokes.
1970s. Polyester/cotton.
($16-24)

Two tone shirt with contrasting
pastel color tones. 1970s.
Polyester/cotton. ($16-24)

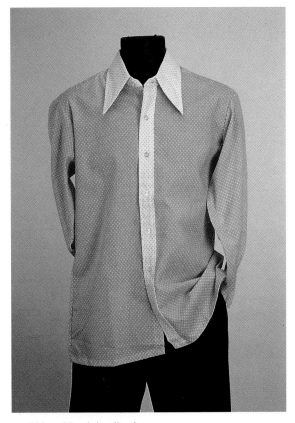

Shirt with mini polka dots.
Polyester/cotton. Late 1960s to
early 1970s. ($16-24)

Star Trek characters
in cartoon format.
Polyester. 1970s.
*Courtesy of Dennie
Dolan.* ($85-125)

Shirt with European courtyard scene. 1970s.
Polyester. ($20-30)

Hot air balloon print. 1970s.
Polyester. *Courtesy of Wear It
Again Sam, Philadelphia.*
($20-30)

Photo print shirt with sports theme.
1970s. Polyester. ($30-35)

Cool Man !!

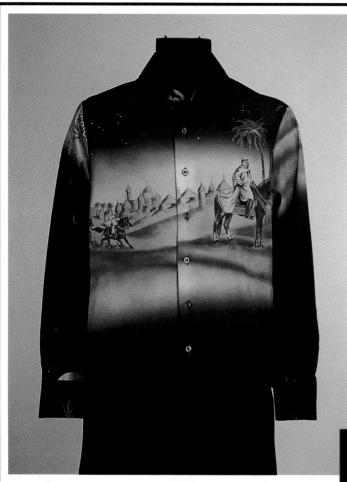

"Arabian Nights " scene. Polyester.
1970s. *Courtesy of Dennie Dolan.*
($40-65)

38

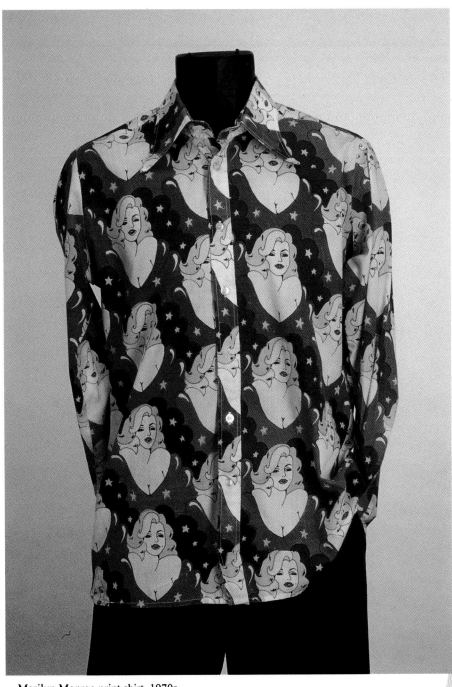

Marilyn Monroe print shirt. 1970s.
Polyester/cotton. ($75-100)

Rappers® brand shirt. Cactus and rabbit print.
Polyester/cotton. 1970s. ($20-30)

Photo print shirt with stage and
screen dancers. 1970s. Polyester.
($25-35)

Photo print shirt with Western mountain scene and waterfall. 1970s. Polyester. *Courtesy of Elizabeth Hine.* ($25-35)

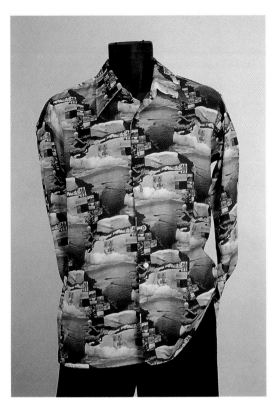

Photo print shirt. Arrow® brand with Joe Namath endorsement. Beach scene with surfers and girls in bikinis. Polyester. 1970s. *Courtesy of Elizabeth Hine.* ($35-50)

Antique car print. 1970s. Polyester. ($20-30)

Abstract patchwork print. 1970s. Polyester. *Courtesy of Wear It Again Sam, Philadelphia.* ($25-35)

Art Nouveau print. 1970s. Polyester. ($25-35)

Vintage scene of men playing volleyball. 1970s. Polyester. *Courtesy of Wear It Again Sam, Philadelphia.* ($30-35)

Print shirt with vintage Arrow shirt advertising. 1970s. Polyester. *Courtesy of Elizabeth Hine.* ($30-35)

Arrow® brand shirt with Joe Namath endorsement. Fields of flowers and rainbows. 1970s. Polyester. *Courtesy of Elizabeth Hine.* ($30-35)

T-shirts

Beginning in the 1950s, but best expressed in the '60s and '70s, T-shirts became a fashion item. Before that, they were just underwear. The unisex look was born. If you were lucky enough to be the same size as your boyfriend or girlfriend, there were many T-shirts, jeans, and jackets that either of you could wear.

T-shirt with silk screen of chimpanzee on front and back. 1970s. Polyester/cotton. ($18-24)

Gorilla behind cityscape. Screen print T-shirt. 1970s. Polyester/rayon. ($25-30)

Youth T-shirt. Gorilla holding girl. Screen print. 1970s. Polyester/cotton. ($25-30)

Teen sweatshirt. Silk-screen of Beatles with facsimile signatures. Copyright 1963. 100 percent Cotton. ($130-160)

44

Cartoon print sweatshirt. Label says "Authentic Monkees Pop-Art Shirt." Copyright 1967. Cotton. ($150-200)

Newspaper print T-shirt, silk screen. 1970s. Polyester/cotton. ($18-20)

"Mork" T-shirt. 1970s. 100 percent cotton. ($20)

Pastel patchwork T-shirt. 1970s. Polyester/cotton. ($16-20)

Denim patchwork print T-shirt. 1970s. Polyester/cotton. ($16-20)

Gray denim and calico patchwork print T-shirt. 1970s. Polyester/cotton. ($16-20)

Stars and stripes heavy cotton T-shirt. 1970s.
Cotton. ($20-25)

Multi striped T-shirts. Polyester/cotton
blends. 1970s. ($15-18)

Striped T-shirt. Polyester/cotton
blends. 1970s. ($15-18)

T-shirt with deep tone stripes. Polyester/
cotton blends. 1970s. ($15-18)

Henley style knit shirts
with checks and stripes.
1970s. Polyester/cotton.
($16-20)

Dee Cee® Rappers® shirt. Three-tone
pullover with collar. 1970s. Polyester/
cotton knit. ($18-22)

Dee Cee® Rappers® shirt. Two-
tone pullover with collar. 1970s.
Polyester/cotton knit. ($18-22)

48

T-shirt with silk screen of working cowboy. 1970s. Polyester. ($20-25)

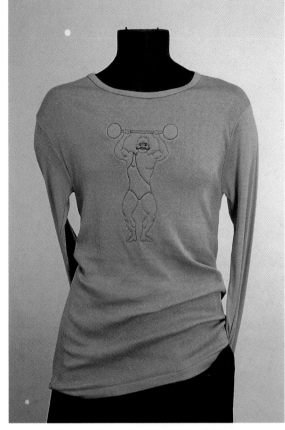

Wrangler® brand pullover with embroidered weight lifter. 1970s. Polyester/cotton. ($30-35)

T-shirt with bike racer. Silk screen. 1970s. Polyester/cotton. ($18-20)

T-shirt with shark and scuba
diver. Photo print. 1970s.
Polyester/rayon. ($20-25)

Surfs Up !

T-shirt with Sorceress and fairy.
Silk screen. 1970s. Polyester/
cotton. ($35-45)

T-shirt with semi-nude woman.
Photo print. 1970s. Textured
polyester. ($40-50)

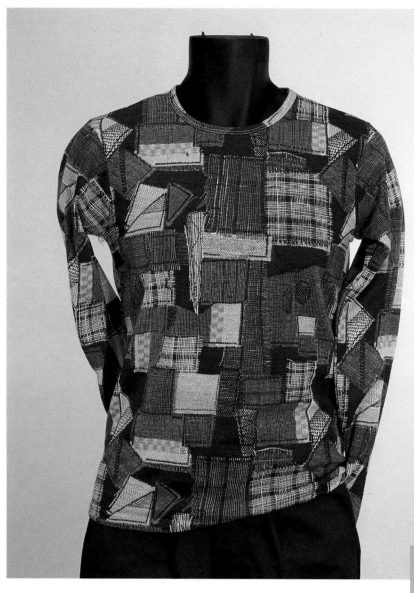

T-shirts with patchwork print. 1970s. Polyester/ cotton. ($18-20)

Pullover T-shirt with dirt bike racers. 1970s. Polyester/ cotton. ($18-24)

T-shirt with Indian in full
headdress on horse. Photo print
1970s. Acrylic. ($25-35)

Long-sleeve pullover with teepee
print. 1970s. Polyester/cotton.
($18-24)

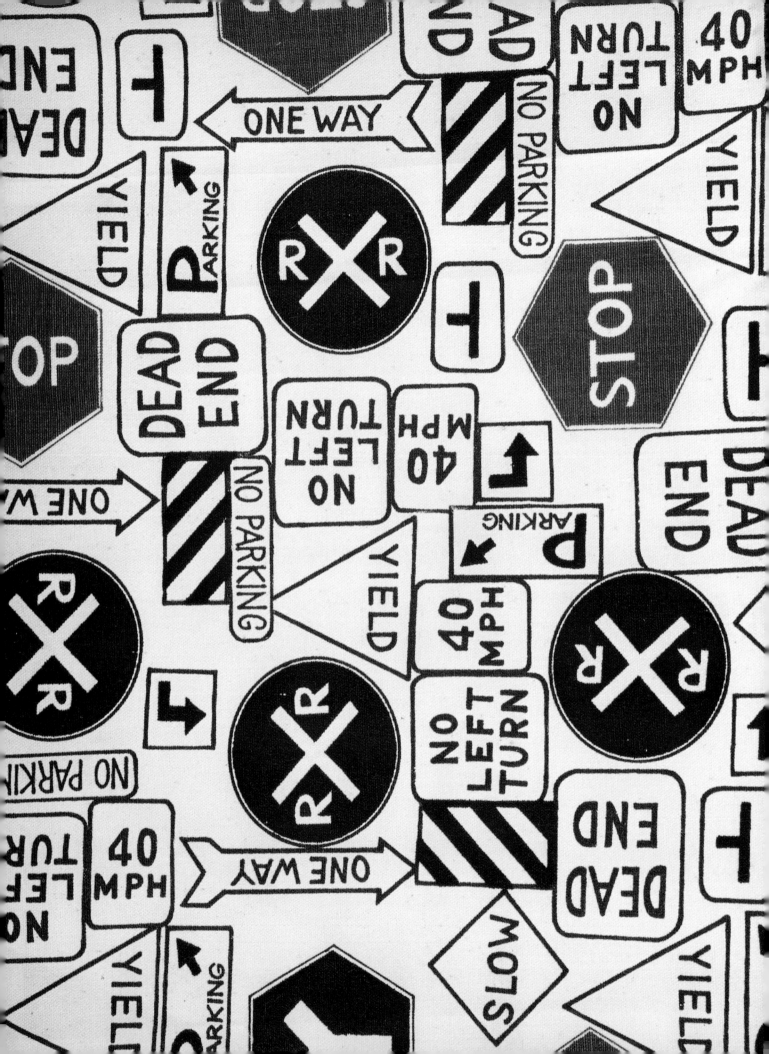

Chapter Two

Cool Pants

Straight Leg Pants

Whether for school or the Friday night hop, Ivy style trousers were an excellent choice. For parties and clubbing, shark skins were better. If they were a really wild color, better yet.

Levi's "Sta-Prest"® taper leg pants. Green twill. Polyester/cotton. Late 1960s. *Courtesy of Wear It Again Sam, Philadelphia.* ($35-45)

Levi's "Sta-Prest Slim Fit"® pants. Canvas weave with brown and blue check. Polyester/cotton. Late 1960s. ($35-45)

Levi's "Sta-Prest Nuvos"® taper leg pants. Brown canvas weave. Polyester/cotton. .Late 1960s. ($35-45)

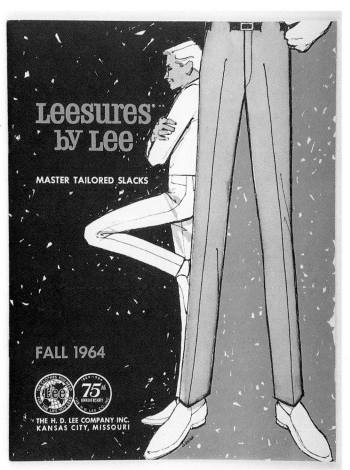

Lee Fastback Leesures®. Brown and green mini-check pants with hidden back pockets for a slimmer look. Polyester/cotton. Late 1960s. *Courtesy of Wear It Again Sam, Philadelphia.* ($30-40)

Lee Leans® taper leg five pocket slacks. Gold and green check. Polyester/cotton. Late 1960s to early 1970s. ($30-40)

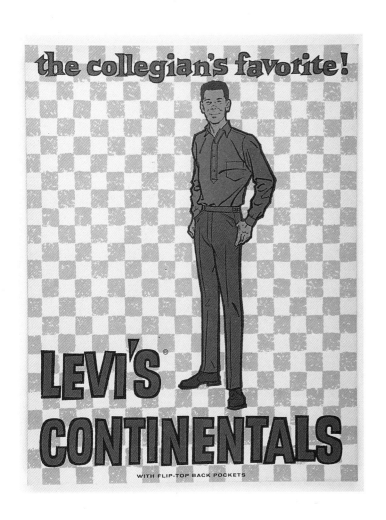

Levi's® "Spikes" and Mark I Continental slacks. Olive green and gold textured cotton. Waist adjustable with button tab. 1960s. ($35-48)

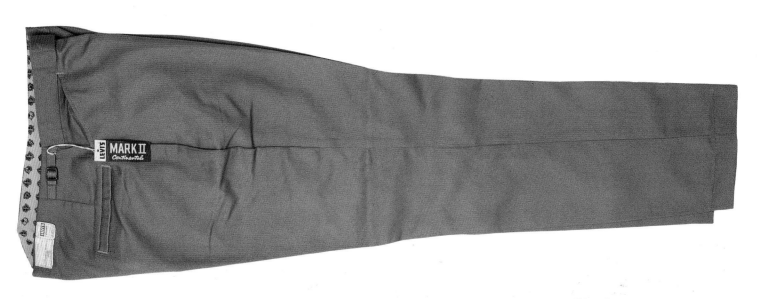

Levi's® Continental Mark II all cotton slacks. Waist size adjustable by side cinches. 1960s. ($35-48)

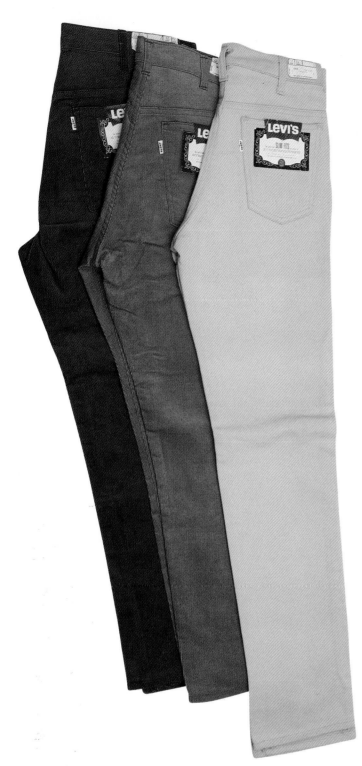

Wrangler® Taper Fit five pocket jeans. Dark brown and black all cotton denim. 1960s. ($35-45)

Levi's® Slim Fit five pocket jeans. All cotton. "Big E" on white tab. Brown and tan corduroy, off-white twills. Late 1960s. ($35-48)

Wrangler® long 'n leans. Black five pocket corduroy jeans. All cotton. 1960s. ($35-48)

Lee Leans® five-pocket taper leg jeans. Tan. Polyester/cotton twills. Early 1970s. ($30-40)

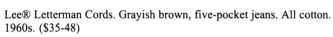

Lee® Letterman Cords. Grayish brown, five-pocket jeans. All cotton. 1960s. ($35-48)

Straight-leg sharkskin dress slacks. Iridescent bronze, steel, and copper with black fleck pattern. Rayon blend. 1960s. ($48-60)

Continental dress trousers. Extended waistband with button closure. Saddle stitching on pockets. Wool and silk blend. Apricot tone-on-tone pattern. Late 1960s to early 1970s. ($48-60)

Straight-leg dress slacks. Extended waistband with buckle and belt loop. Saddle-stitched detail on pockets. Wool and silk. Bright tangerine. Late 1960s to early 1970s. ($48-60)

Sharkskin dress trousers. Ivy style with piped pockets. Rayon/acetate blend. Canary yellow. 1960s. ($48-60)

Straight-leg dress trousers. Extended waistband with buckle. Saddle stitching and watch pocket. Polyester/rayon blend. Red. Late 1960s to early 1970s. *Courtesy of Wear It Again Sam, Philadelphia.* ($48-60)

Straight-leg dress trousers. Extended waistband with buckle. Saddle-stitched detail on pockets. Wool and silk blend. Plum. Late 1960s to early 1970s. ($48-60)

Taper-leg dress trousers. Woven windowpane design. Polyester/rayon blend. 1960s. *Courtesy of Wear It Again Sam, Philadelphia.* ($35-45)

Wild Things

Bell bottoms came on the fashion scene in the late '60s and stayed popular right through the mid '70s. They got their name from—you guessed it—the bell shape of the leg. While originally worn with huaraches and a headband, eventually everyone from tots to guys like my brother would eventually own a pair. No one ever thought this style would last as long as it did, and no one ever wanted it to come back once it was gone. Guess what?

Peter Max® jeans by Wrangler®.
All cotton. Late 1960s to early
1970s ($175-275)

Wild Thing

62

Maverick® flare jeans.
Brushed cotton. 1970s.
($45-65)

Maverick® flare jeans. Black with white patch
pockets and waistband. All cotton. Early 1970s.
Courtesy of Wear It Again Sam, Philadelphia.
($35-55)

Wrangler® low-cut
flares. All cotton.
1970s. ($45-65)

Maverick® women's flare leg jeans. Stars and peace doves. All cotton. Early 1970s. ($65-95)

Maverick® Blue Bell® flare-leg jeans. Brushed cotton. 1970s *Courtesy of Wear It Again Sam, Philadelphia.* ($40-60)

Wrangler® flare leg jeans. Patchwork pattern with solid patch pockets, waistband and flare. All cotton. Late 1960s to early 1970s. *Courtesy of Wear It Again Sam, Philadelphia.* ($40-50)

Maverick® "Big Flare Leg" jeans. Dark denim with light denim insert down leg and at pockets. Polyester/cotton blend. Early 1970s. *Courtesy of Wear It Again Sam, Philadelphia.* ($40-50)

bell bottoms

For the "In Group" that is really "with it"

With the New Flare

AQUEDUCT

another NATIONALLY FAMOUS

REIDBORD product

Brushed cotton flare jeans. Grommets on front pockets. Early 1970s. ($45-65)

Bell Bottoms

Model wearing flare-
leg jeans with
geometric pattern.
Button fly. Patch
pockets on front and
back. All cotton. Late
'60s to early '70s.
($45-65)

Maverick® women's
flare jeans. Tennis
racket print. All
cotton. 1970s.
*Courtesy of Wear It
Again Sam, Philadel-
phia.* ($35-45)

66

Button-fly bell-bottom jeans. Inset pockets on front. All cotton. Late 1960s. *Courtesy of Wear It Again Sam, Philadelphia.* ($35-45)

Button-fly bell-bottom jeans. All cotton. Late 1960s. *Courtesy of Wear It Again Sam, Philadelphia.* ($35-45)

Lee Riders® Boot Cut jeans. Polyester/cotton blend. 1970s. ($35-45)

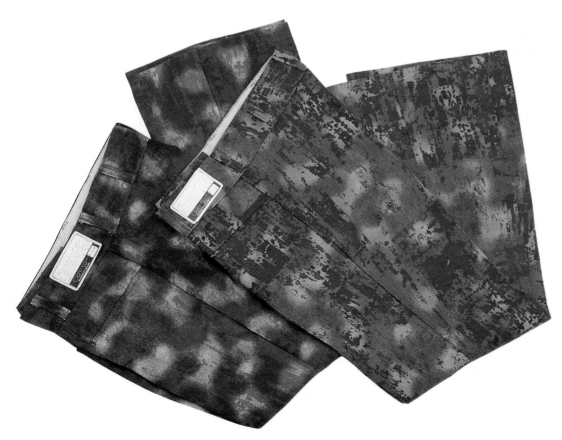

Flare-leg slacks. Wide waistband. Polyester / cotton blend. Early 1970s. ($35-45)

Flare Legs

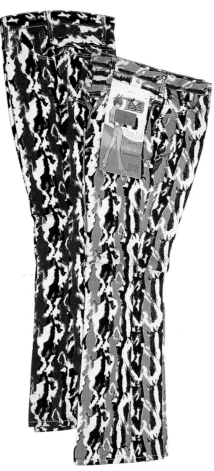

Maverick® Blue Bell® women's flare jeans. All cotton. Late 1960s to early 1970s. ($35-45)

Maverick® women's jeans. Farm scene on flare leg. All cotton. 1960s. ($40-60)

Women's flare-leg pants. Western-style belt loops and back yoke. Indian needlepoint design. Rayon/cotton blend. Late 1960s to early 1970s. ($35-45)

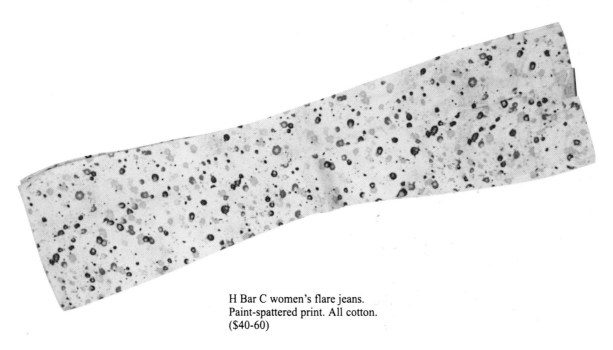

H Bar C women's flare jeans. Paint-spattered print. All cotton. ($40-60)

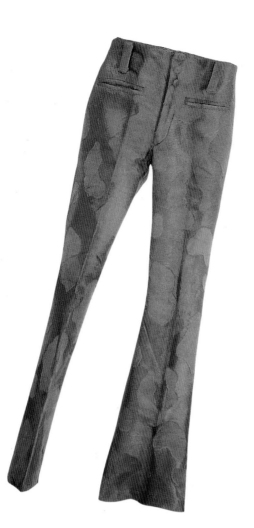

Flare-leg pants. Funky faux fur. Acrylic/cotton blend. 1970s. ($45-60)

Unisex bell bottoms. Rayon velour. Wine color. 1960s. ($40-45)

Maverick® flare jeans. Maverick® logo and knotted-rope design. All cotton. ($35-45)

Girl's flares. Daisy print. All cotton. 1960s. ($15-22)

Girl's bell bottoms. "Hippie" print. All cotton. 1960s. ($15-22)

Bell Bottoms

Children's flares. Cloth tag says, "The Partridge Family® by Kate Greenaway." All cotton. 1970s. ($45-65)

Children's flares. Partridge Family® bus print. David Cassidy "official" fan club membership information on paper label. Designed by Kate Greenaway. 1970s. ($50-65)

70

Hillbilly brand women's flare jeans. Slanted zippered pockets and Western-style yoke. Brushed cotton. 1970s. *Courtesy of Wear It Again Sam, Philadelphia.* ($35-45)

Unisex bell bottoms. Patch pockets with zipper and ring closure. Brushed cotton. 1970s. *Courtesy of Wear It Again Sam, Philadelphia.* ($35-45)

Women's flare-leg jeans. Double zipper at waistband. Brushed cotton. 1970s. *Courtesy of Wear It Again Sam, Philadelphia.* ($35-45)

Women's Maverick® flare jeans. Polyester/cotton blend. Early 1970s. *Courtesy of Wear It Again Sam, Philadelphia.* ($35-45)

Flare-leg pants. Button fly. Cargo pocket at knee. All cotton. 1970s. ($35-45)

Maverick® bell-bottom jeans. Contrast stitching over raw edge on yoke, pockets and belt loops. All cotton. Early 1970s. *Courtesy of Wear It Again Sam, Philadelphia.* ($35-45)

Woodstock

Maverick® velour flare-leg jeans. Cargo pockets on front with three-snap closure. All cotton. Early 1970s. ($35-45)

Velour flare-leg pants. Cuffed patch pockets with buttons on front. All cotton. Early 1970s. ($35-45)

Studded denim flares. All cotton. 1970s. ($45-65)

74

Dress pants with accordion pleat flare and unusual front closure. Rayon/acetate blend. 1960s. ($45-65)

Maverick® dress flares. Textured fabric. Polyester/rayon blend. Early 1970s. *Courtesy of Wear It Again Sam, Philadelphia.* ($35-45)

Brushed cotton hip huggers. Slit-front pockets. Yoke front and back. All cotton. Cocoa brown. 1960s. ($35-45)

Model wearing low-rise bell bottoms. Snap fly. Cotton. 1960s. ($35-45)

Hip hugger flares. Button fly front. Four-button closure. Brushed cotton. 1960s. ($35-45)

Campus® brand low-rise jeans. Label reads "Western Chop Top." Brushed cotton. 1960s. ($35-45)

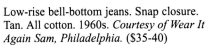

Low-rise bell-bottom jeans. Snap closure. Tan. All cotton. 1960s. *Courtesy of Wear It Again Sam, Philadelphia.* ($35-40)

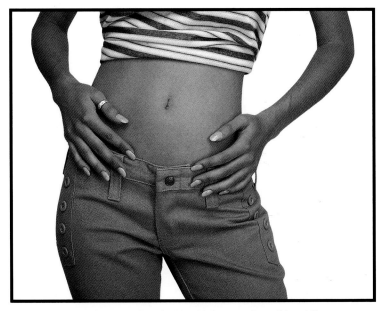

Model wearing low-rise flare jeans with button trim at hips. All cotton. Tan. 1960s. ($35-45)

Campus® "Super Low Cut" jeans. Plain front for that trim look. Richly textured corduroy. All cotton. 1960s. *Courtesy of Wear It Again Sam, Philadelphia.* ($35-45)

Hip Huggers

Wrangler® "Big Bell" denim jeans. Zipper fly with front patch pockets. All cotton. Early 1970s. ($35-45)

Wrangler® women's "Big Bell" jeans. Zipper fly with snap waist. Patch pockets on front. Bottom of flare measures wider than waist. Cotton. 1970s. ($35-40)

Elephant bells with inset front pockets and wide belt loops. Zipper fly and snap waist closure. Brushed cotton. Early 1970s. *Courtesy of Wear It Again Sam, Philadelphia.* ($35-45)

Washington Rappers Goliath Bell jeans. Patch pockets and zipper fly. Flare measures 31inches. Tag says "Advertised in Playboy." Brushed denim. Early 1970s. ($35-45)

Elephant Bells

"Super Low Rise Elephant Bells." Front inset pockets. All cotton. Purple. 1970s. ($35-45)

Maverick® "Big Bell Baggies"® Patch pockets on front and back. Zipper fly and snap front closure. Polyester/cotton. 1970s. ($35-45)

Baggies and Disco Flares

Is there anything redeeming to say about polyester pants? Well, the first thing is that they didn't wrinkle. The second is that, if you dripped gravy on them, there was no need to rush for a towel. It would just roll off. The bad news was, you couldn't really wipe your hands on them at dinner either. Men tried this and failed for years. The third is that you could launder them with your socks and towels and they would come out looking as sharp as the day you bought them. I never thought I'd come up with three good things to say about them. There is no fourth redeeming virtue.

Baggy dress pants. Polyester/rayon blend. 1970s. *Courtesy of Wear It Again Sam, Philadelphia.* ($35-45)

Maverick® Baggies. Polyester/ rayon blend. 1970s. *Courtesy of Wear It Again Sam, Philadelphia.* ($35-45)

Mr. Wrangler® Baggies. Polyester/cotton blend. 1970s. ($35-45)

Unisex Baggies. Corduroy. All cotton. 1970s. ($35-45)

Maverick® brand Baggies. Scoop-front pockets and rear patch pockets. Polyester/cotton blend. 1970s. *Courtesy of Wear It Again Sam, Philadelphia.* ($35-45)

Baggy jeans. Polyester/cotton twills. 1970s. ($35-45)

Double knit flares. Textured fabric with embroidered designs on front pockets. Bunny buttons on 3 ½ inch waistband. Polyester. 1970s. ($40-60)

Double-knit dress flares. Extended waist with single belt loop. Black with silver threading. Polyester. 1970s. ($50-65)

Double-knit flared pants. Blue-and-white diamond pattern with red. Two-inch beltless waistband. Polyester. 1970s. ($35-45)

Dress flare pants. Unusual graduated color scheme. Polyester. 1970s. ($50-55)

Double-knit dress flares. Herringbone design. Polyester. 1970s. ($35-45)

Textured double-knit dress flares. Gray, white, and black abstract design. 1970s. *Courtesy of Wear It Again Sam, Philadelphia.* ($40-50)

Double-knit dress flares. Abstract design. Polyester. 1970s. *Courtesy of Wear It Again Sam, Philadelphia.* ($35-45)

Double-knit dress flares. Bright floral pattern with gold and silver thread running through design. Polyester. 1970s. *Courtesy of Wear It Again Sam, Philadelphia.* ($40-55)

Wet-look dress flares. Three-inch extended waistband and red topstitching. Polyester. 1970s. ($55-65)

84

Double-knit dress flares. Pink and charcoal diamond pattern. Polyester. 1970s. *Courtesy of Wear It Again Sam, Philadelphia.* ($35-45)

Double-knit dress flares. Extended waist. Abstract pattern. Polyester. 1970s. *Courtesy of Wear It Again Sam, Philadelphia.* ($45-60)

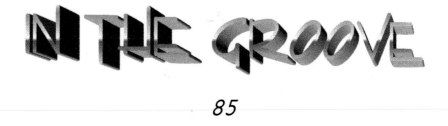

Chapter Three

Skimpy Swimwear and Surfin' Shorts

As one of the longest-lasting fashion trends of this century, bikinis have always left less and less to the imagination. Before bikinis, men had better things to do than to hang around at the beach. Since then, cooler and volleyball net sales have increased dramatically.

Groups like the Beach Boys and Jan Dean helped popularize surfing as a fashion and a lifestyle. You could look like a surfer without actually being one. Did you have a woody and surfboard?

Campus® "Surf A' Go-Go" shirt. Tapered body with side slits and cigarette pocket on left sleeve. Cloth neck tag has two fancy embroidered surfboards. Cotton/rayon blend. 1960s. ($45-65)

The inside of this tag is a printed guide to "surf jargon."

Henley style surf shirts. All cotton. 1960s. ($18-22)

"Grubb Stuff" pants by Robert Bruce®. "Peace and Love" design. 1960s. 100 percent cotton. ($25-30)

Men's surfer shorts. Bright floral print. Eyelet and ties at waist. Polyester/cotton. 1960s. ($20-30)

Men's surfer shorts. Pocket on side of leg. Green surfer print. Cotton. 1960s. *Courtesy of Wear It Again Sam, Philadelphia.* ($25-30)

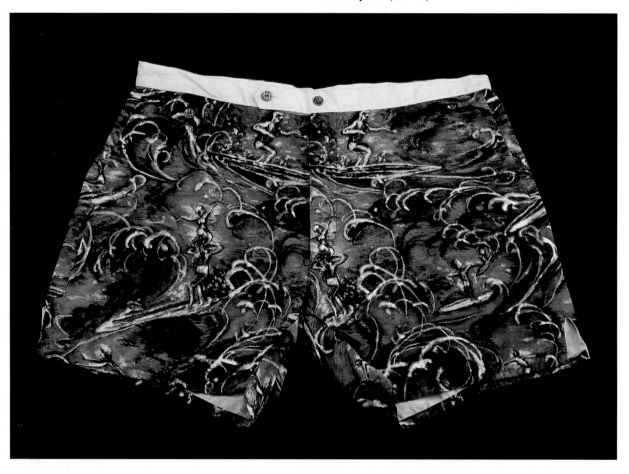

Jams with Tiki print.
Drawstring waist. 100
percent cotton. 1960s.
($20-30)

Swim trunks by Campus®. Madras
plaid. Eyelet and tie. Cotton. 1960's.
($18-24)

Swim trunks by Campus®.
Black and white. Nylon.
1960's. ($18-24)

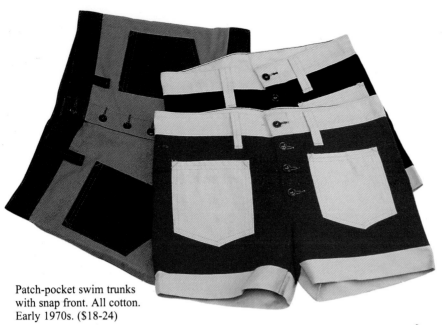

Patch-pocket swim trunks
with snap front. All cotton.
Early 1970s. ($18-24)

Wrangler® swim trunks. "Yes
and No" allover print. All
cotton. Early 1970s. ($20-24)

Men's bathing trunks. Blue patchwork and Madras plaid. Polyester.
1970s. ($18-24)

Men's bathing trunks. Green-
and-brown patchwork design.
Polyester. 1960s. ($18-24)

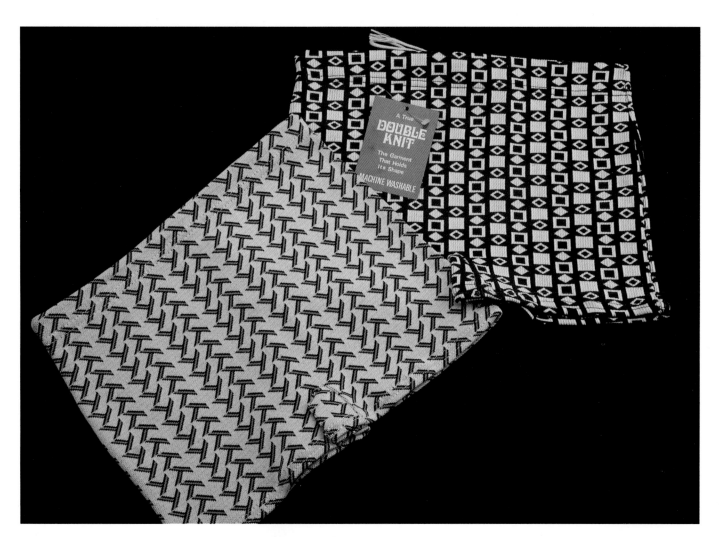

Men's double-knit swim trunks. Yellow-and-blue geometric patterns. Nylon. 1970s. ($18-24)

Men's swim wear by Campus®. Patchwork plaid. 100 percent cotton. 1970s. ($20-30)

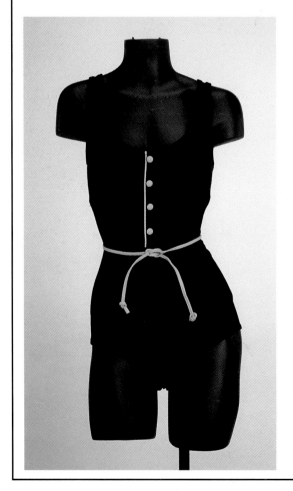

One-piece bathing suits with vinyl buttons and tie belt. Nylon. 1960s *Courtesy of Wear It Again Sam, Philadelphia.* ($30-45)

One-piece bathing suit by Catalina®. Black background with brightly colored flowers. Polyester. Late 1960s. ($30-45)

One piece bathing suits with revealing opening. Nylon. 1960s. ($30-45)

"Teeny weeny polka dot bikinis…" Nylon. Late 1960s to early 1970s. *Courtesy of Wear It Again Sam, Philadelphia.* ($30-36)

Bikini with halter-style top. Multi-colored geometric print. Cotton. Late 1960s to early 1970s. ($30-36)

"Modified" bikini. Large red polka dots. Nylon. 1960s. *Courtesy of Wear It Again Sam, Philadelphia.* ($30-36)

Model wearing bikini accentuated with large buckle. Bright yellow. Polyester. 1970s. ($30-36)

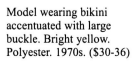

Two-piece bathing suit with red patent belt. Plaid. Cotton. 1960s *Courtesy of Wear It Again Sam, Philadelphia.* ($30-36)

Sporty two-piece bathing suit. High cut bottoms with belted waist. Red with white trim. Nylon. 1960s. ($30-36)

Two-piece swim suit with a nautical look. Striped top and lace-up waist. Nylon. Late 1960s to early 1970s. ($30-36)

Bright floral bathing suit. Green trim at waist. Cotton. 1960s. ($30-36)

Polka dot swim suit. Cotton 1960s. ($30-36)

Day-glo bikinis with embossed
diamond pattern. Cotton. 1960s
($30-36)

LET IT ALL HANG OUT

Daisy print bikinis with
hearts at bust and hips.
Polyester/cotton. Late 1960s.
($30-36)

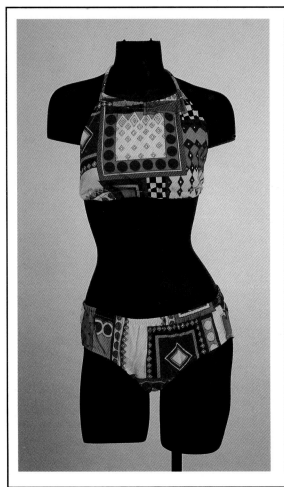
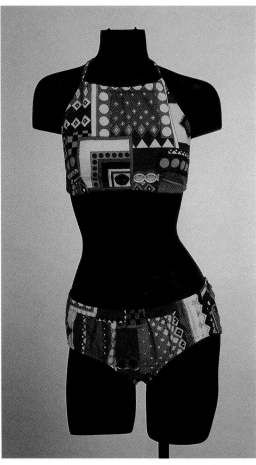

Two-piece swim suits with high-cut halter top. Neon geometric prints. Cotton. Late 1960s to early 1970s. ($30-36)

Bikinis with eyelets and ties on waist and halter. Nylon. 1960s. ($30-36)

98

Bikinis with front-tie halter top. Bold background with floral design. Cotton. Late 1960s to early 1970s. ($30-36)

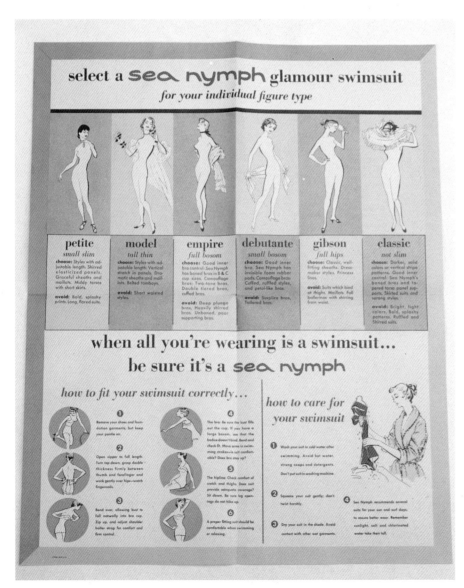

Dresses

Patio Prints

Grab your flip flops, the charcoal briquettes, and the Zippo lighter fluid. These dresses were the perfect daytime attire for those less formal occasions. A barbeque, an afternoon of shopping, or a chat over the fence were ideal situations to wear a shift.

"Patio Print" shift dresses with front zip. Late '60s to early '70s. 100 percent cotton. ($24-30)

Roll collar paper dresses. "Wash a few times, then throw away." Polyester. 1960s. ($25-40)

Polka dot print dress with inverted pleat from yoke to hem. 1960s. Cotton. ($24-36)

Sleeveless shift dress. Red-and-blue bandanna paisley. Late 1960s. Cotton. ($24-36)

Model wearing "curvaceous" shift dress. Jeanie® by Blue Bell® brand. Late 1960s. Cotton knit. ($28-36)

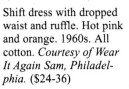

Shift dress with dropped waist and ruffle. Hot pink and orange. 1960s. All cotton. *Courtesy of Wear It Again Sam, Philadelphia.* ($24-36)

Hawaiian sundress with ruffle at neckline. Label says "Sun Fashions of Hawaii." 1960s. Cotton. ($45)

Culotte shift dress with bow at dropped waist. Quilted stand-up collar. Abstract floral pattern. Polyester/cotton. Late 1960s to early 1970s. ($24-36)

"Wet Look" sleeveless skimmer. Paisley print. 1960s. Acetate. ($30-36)

103

A-line skimmers with princess seams. Bow at V-neck. Bright floral pattern. Late '60s early '70s. Polyester/cotton. ($24-36)

Sleeveless culotte dress. White accent at neck and pleat. Floral print. Late '60s to early '70s. Cotton/rayon. *Courtesy of Wear It Again Sam, Philadelphia.* ($24-36)

Pant dress with center panel and side slits. Daisy print with hot pink. 1960s. Polyester/cotton. ($24-36)

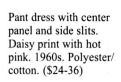

104

Cullote shift with "Pucci Look" butterfly print in orange, hot pink, and purple. 1960s. Acetate. ($24-36)

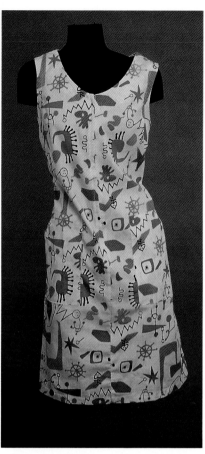

Front-zip shift dress. "Miro type" print. Hot pink, lime, and orange. 1960s. Cotton. ($24-36)

Sleeveless shift dress with ties at shoulder and dropped waist. Bright polka dot print. 1960s. Cotton. ($35-45)

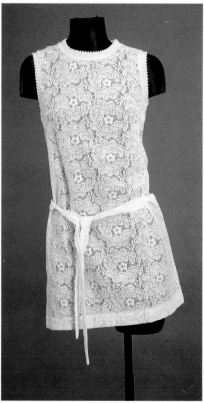

Lace mini dresses. Late 1960s to early 1970s. Acrylic. ($24-36)

Goin' Out Dresses

In the '60s and '70s dresses weren't nearly as popular as coordinates and pant suits. But if you had to go to a wedding, visit your grandmother, or were asked to a prom, something a little fancier was in order.

"Lounger" with quilted skirt. Peasant-style top. 1970s. Polyester. ($30-45)

Hostess dress with floral quilted skirt. "Wet look" top. 1970s. Polyester. ($30-45)

Linen-look sheath dress
with polka dot ruffles at
sleeve. Purple. 1960s.
Rayon/polyester. ($40-50)

Granny style dress with bright floral print and
ruffle at bottom. Late 1960s. Acetate. ($35-45)

Nehru-style shift dress with bell
sleeves. Brightly colored paisley
print. Challis. 1960s. *Courtesy of
Barbara Schuette*. ($30-45)

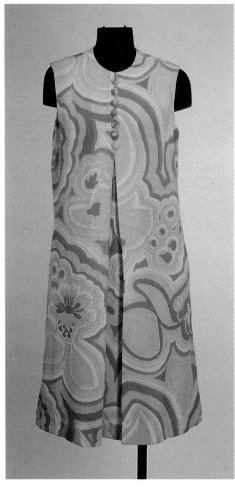

Sleeveless shift dress. Covered buttons with loops and inverted pleat. Orange and yellow. 1960s. Rayon/polyester. ($35-45)

Long-sleeve mini dress. Yellow-and-brown stripes at bottom of sleeves and hem. 1960s. Polyester. *Courtesy of Barbara Schuette.* ($30-45)

Black knit shift dress with checker board sleeves and sash that can be worn at neck or waist. 1960s. Cotton. ($45-65)

Left: Animal print sheath dress. Stand up collar and three quarter sleeves. 1960s. Acetate. ($40-55)

Right: Crushed velvet dress with tie-dye pattern and front slit. Nehru collar. 1960s. Rayon/acrylic blend. *Courtesy of Barbara Schuette.* ($75-110)

Bottom left: Snakeskin print lounging robe with front snap closure. Polyester. Late 1960s to early 1970s. ($30-36)

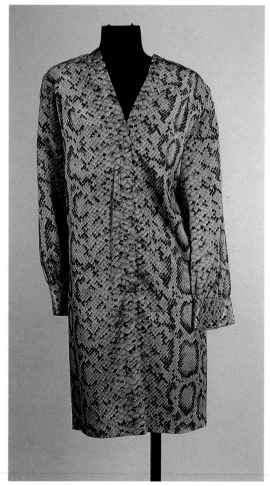

109

Chapter Five

All The Rest

Skirts, Shorts, and Jeans

Parents hated mini skirts with a passion, but young girls loved them for several reasons. They were easily hidden under "acceptable skirts" on a Friday night. Turning older mid-length skirts into minis could be done quickly with a needle and thread. Denim skirts required even less work than that. A pair of scissors and cycle in the washer-dryer did the job.

Maxi shirt. Cotton velvet with bright floral patchwork print. Cotton. 1960s. ($25-35)

Mid-length A-line skirt with large front zipper. Cotton corduroy. Late 1960s. ($24-30)

Mod mini-skirt. Yellow-and-navy checkerboard design. Vinyl. 1960s. ($35)

"Hot Pant Skirts." Polyester/
cotton. Early 1970s. ($24-30)

Hot Pants

"School Girl" style mini skirts. Brown and green plaids. Acrylic/rayon acetate. Late 1960s. ($22-28)

Mini skirt with vinyl belt. Circle print. Orange and yellow. 1960s. Cotton. ($24-30)

Photo 5/1, Chapter 12/11,

Women's belted rain slickers. 1970s. Nylon. ($20-24)

Casual women's jacket with
patch pockets. Antique
railroad print. 1970s. Cotton.
($24-30)

"Route 66" snap-front jacket.
Early 1970s. Cotton. ($30-36)

114

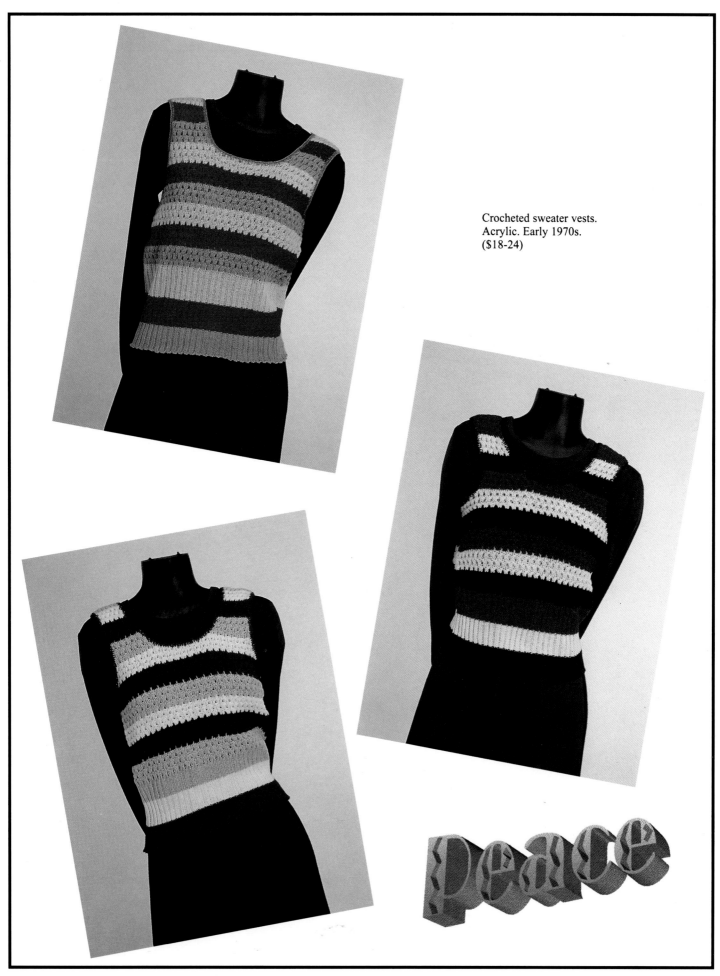

Crocheted sweater vests.
Acrylic. Early 1970s.
($18-24)

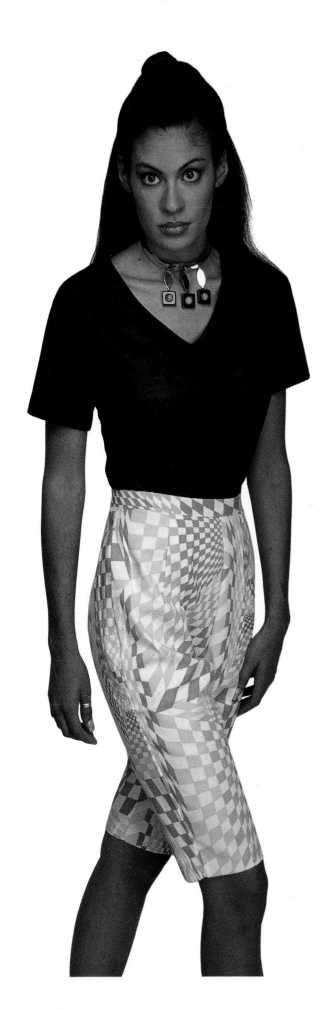

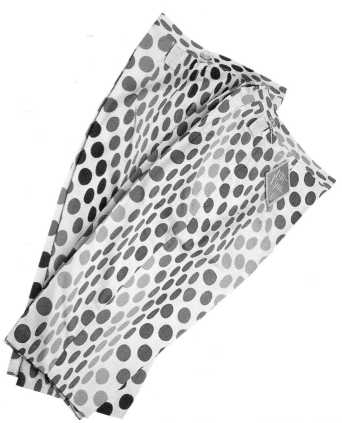

Women's knee pants in bright polka dot prints. Cotton. 1960s. ($30-36)

Women's knee pants with side zip. Bold abstract pattern. 100 percent cotton. 1960s. ($30-36)

Model wearing knee pants in yellow-and-orange op-art print. Cotton. 1960s. ($30-36)

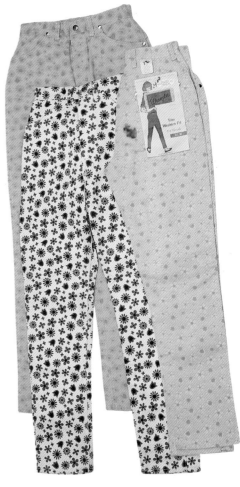

Maverick® "Trim western cut jeans." Bright floral pattern. 100 percent cotton corduroy. 1960s. ($30-35)

Wrangler® "Trim western cut jeans. Daisy prints. 100 percent cotton. 1960s. ($30-35)

Leopard-print capri pants with belt. Corduroy. 100 percent cotton. 1960s. ($45-60)

Stretchy Tops

The idea with poly blouses and scoop neck T-shirts is that they were tight fitting. A casual fashion with jeans, skirts, or hot pants, they were sometimes worn by girls with bad Farrah Fawcett hairdos.

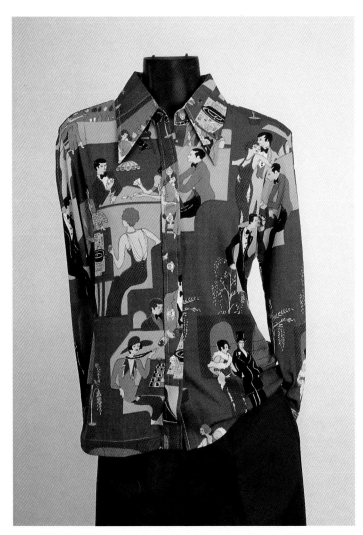

Poly blouse depicting "Roaring Twenties". Beige. 1970s. Nylon. *Courtesy of Wear It Again Sam, Philadelphia.* ($22-28)

Brightly colored floral blouse 1970s. Polyester. ($22-28)

Blouse with geometric design bordered in black. Polyester. 1970s. ($22-28)

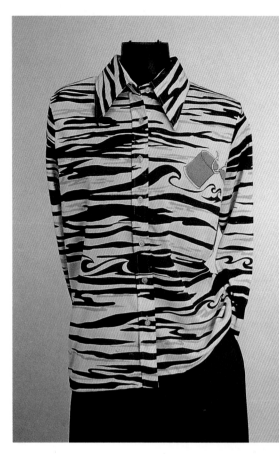

Blouse with "fisherman" theme. 1970s. Polyester. ($35)

Vera® blouse with colorful
butterfly print. Side vents.
1970s. Cotton. ($30-35)

Model wearing blouse with goldfish detail
on back. 1970s. Polyester. ($20-25)

Pullover with "Red Hot Heart" silk-screen. 1970s. Cotton. ($20-24)

Pullover with "Chained Heart" silk-screen. 1970s. Cotton. ($20-24)

123

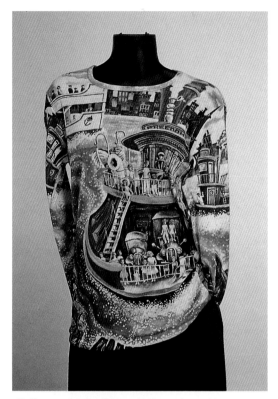

Pullover with families enjoying a ferry ride. 1970s. Polyester. ($20-24)

Pullover with "Eat Your Heart Out … Mine's Gone" silk-screen. Hot pink. 1970s. Nylon. ($18-24)

Pullover with multi-colored patchwork design. 1970s. 100 percent cotton. ($20-24)

Bubble gum scoop-neck tops in pastel colors. 1970s. Nylon. *Courtesy of Wear It Again Sam, Philadelphia.* ($20-24)

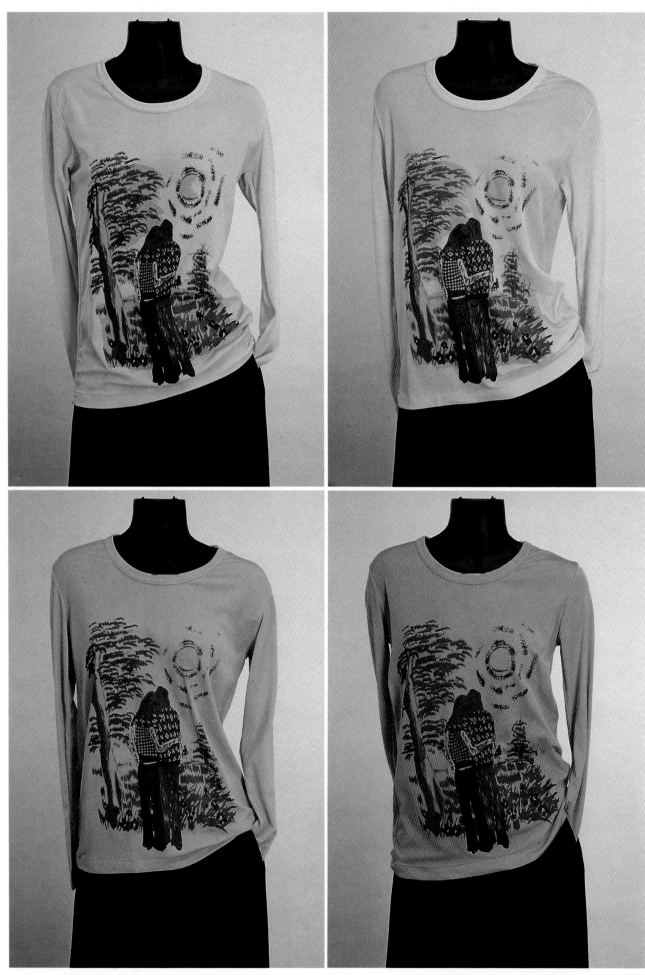

126

Scoop-neck pullovers with
bold diagonal stripes and
floral prints. 1970s. Nylon.
($20-24)

Opposite page:
Scoop-neck tops with lovers
embracing. 1970s. Nylon. ($20-24)

Boldly printed scoop-neck pull-overs. 1970s. Nylon. *Courtesy of Wear It Again Sam, Philadelphia.* ($20-24)

Scoop necks with a "nervous"
zigzag print. 1970s. Nylon.
($20-25)

Wrangler® brand pullover with track runners. 1970s. Polyester/cotton. ($22-26)

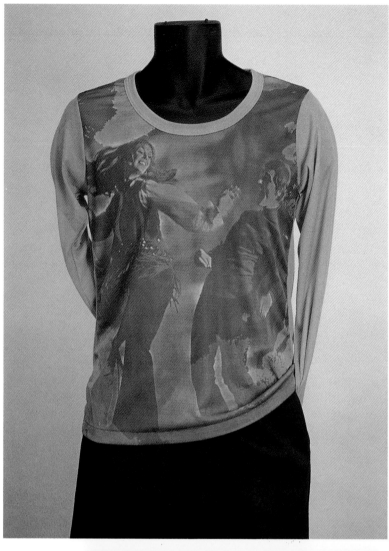

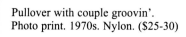
Pullover with couple groovin'.
Photo print. 1970s. Nylon. ($25-30)

Pullover with couple embracing
under umbrella. Photo print.
1970s. Nylon. ($25-30)

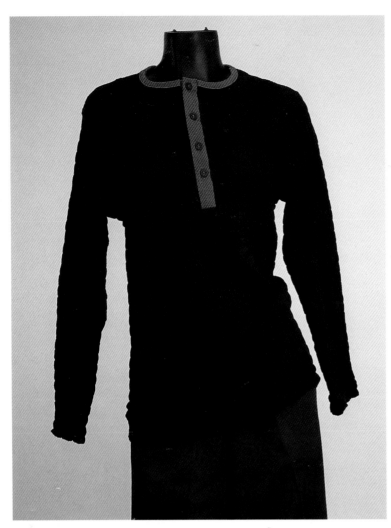

"Pucker knit" pullover by
Campus®. Brown with hot pink
trim. Polyester/cotton blend.
1970s. ($18-24)

Knit shirts with laced
front placket and pocket
on left sleeve. 1970s. 100
percent cotton. ($18-24)

Pullover with double slant
zippers at neck. 1970s. Stretch
nylon. ($18-24)

Knit pullover. Red, white,
and blue with stars. 1970s.
Polyester/cotton blend.
($18-24)

133

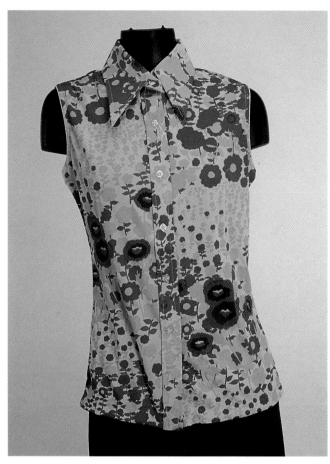
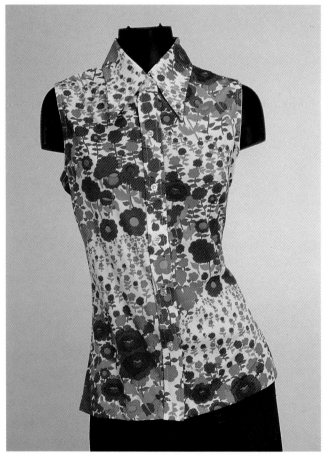

Sleeveless blouses with vivid floral prints. 1970s. Polyester. ($18-24)

134

Blouses with deep
pointed collar. Vivid
tropical prints. 1970s.
Stretch polyester.
($18-24)

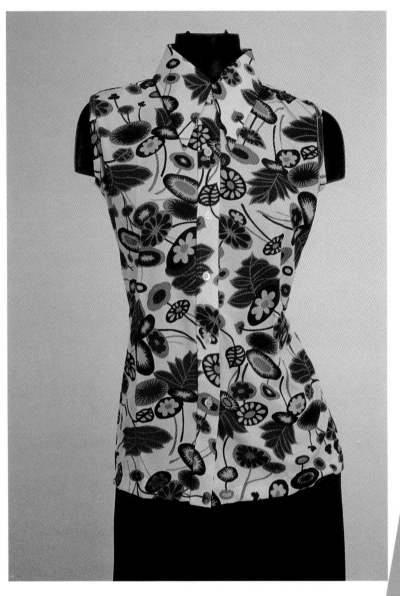

"Funky floral" sleeveless blouses. Polyester. Late 1960s to early 1970s. ($18-24)

136

Sheer blouse by Ship 'n Shore®. Stars on black background. Polyester/ cotton blend. 1970s. ($24-30)

Casual sleeveless blouses. Polyester/ cotton blend. 1970s. ($24-30)

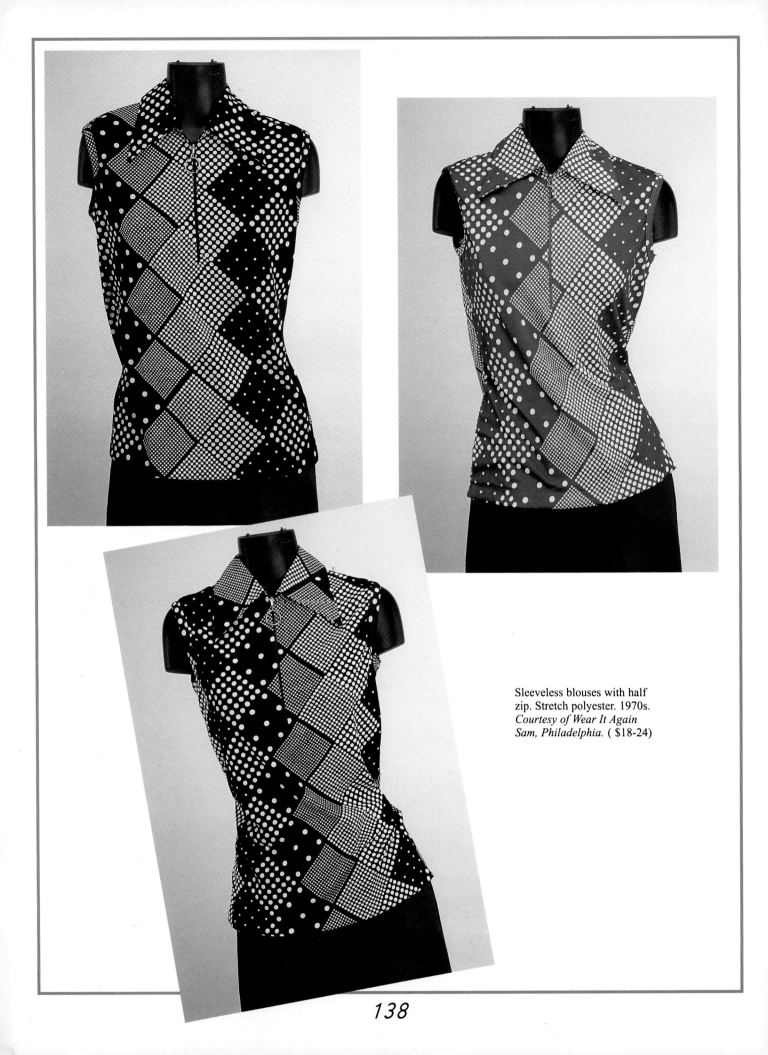

Sleeveless blouses with half
zip. Stretch polyester. 1970s.
*Courtesy of Wear It Again
Sam, Philadelphia.* ($18-24)

T-shirts and Tanks

Need some bubble gum fashion for an Osmonds, Bobby Sherman, or Cowsills concert? A few of these would qualify. The look definitely appealed to the younger crowd.

Model wearing striped rib knit with hot pants. 1970s. Polyester/nylon. ($18-24)

Rib knit tops in solid colors. 1970s. Green, rust, blue. Polyester/nylon. ($18-22)

Striped rib knits with back
zipper and front placket.
1970s. Polyester/nylon.
($18-24)

140

Girl's ribbed knit T-shirt. "Vinnie Barberino" silk-screen. Acrylic. 1970s. ($35-45)

Girl's ribbed knit T-shirt. "Welcome Back Kotter Sweathogs" silk-screen. Acrylic. 1970s. ($35-45)

Knit T-shirts. Contrasting
sleeves and stripes. 1970s.
Polyester/cotton blend.
($16 20)

142

French T-shirt. "Blue Monday" embroidered on front. Blue. 1970s. Nylon. ($20-24)

French T-shirt. "Whens Day ?" embroidered on front. Lime green. 1970s. Nylon. ($20-24)

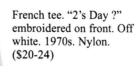

French tee. "2's Day ?" embroidered on front. Off white. 1970s. Nylon. ($20-24)

T-shirt with sexy "Can-can dancers" on front and back. White. 1970s. Nylon. ($28-35)

144

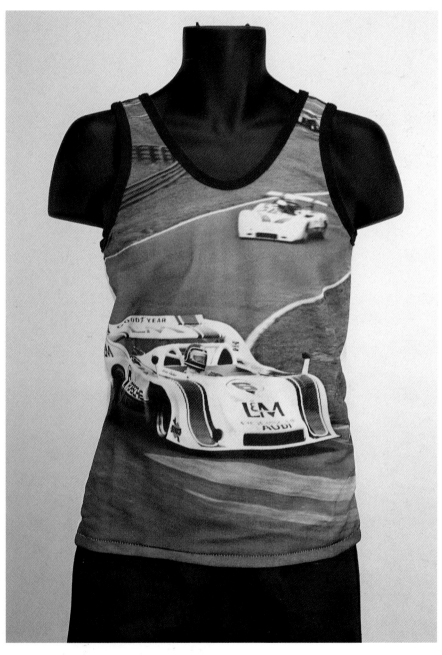

Tank top. Photo print of Indy race cars. 1970s. 100 percent polyester. ($16-20)

Newspaper print tank tops. 1970s. Polyester/cotton. ($16-20)

146

Hanes® printed tank top with solid color binding at armholes
and neck. 1970s. Polyester/cotton. ($14-18)

Model wearing tank top with
men's bathing trunks for a
contemporary summer look.

147

Woman's tank tops. Cloth appliqué with machine embroidery, clothes hanging on the line. 1970s. 100 percent nylon. ($20-26)

Woman's tank top. Cloth appliqué with machine embroidery, "Kiss Me" - "Hug Me". 1970s. Stretch nylon. ($20-26)

149

Woman's tank top. Paris street scene. Peach. 1970s. Stretch nylon. ($24)

Halters, Tube Tops and Sizzling Hot Pants

These were absolutely shocking when they first came on the scene. "What's this younger generation coming to?" Stashed in a purse, you could change into them in the back seat of a Volkswagen or at a girlfriend's house. They were at their best when worn with go-go boots, platform shoes, or bare feet.

Reversible halter tops with collars. Floral and geometric prints. 1970s. Polyester. ($20-25)

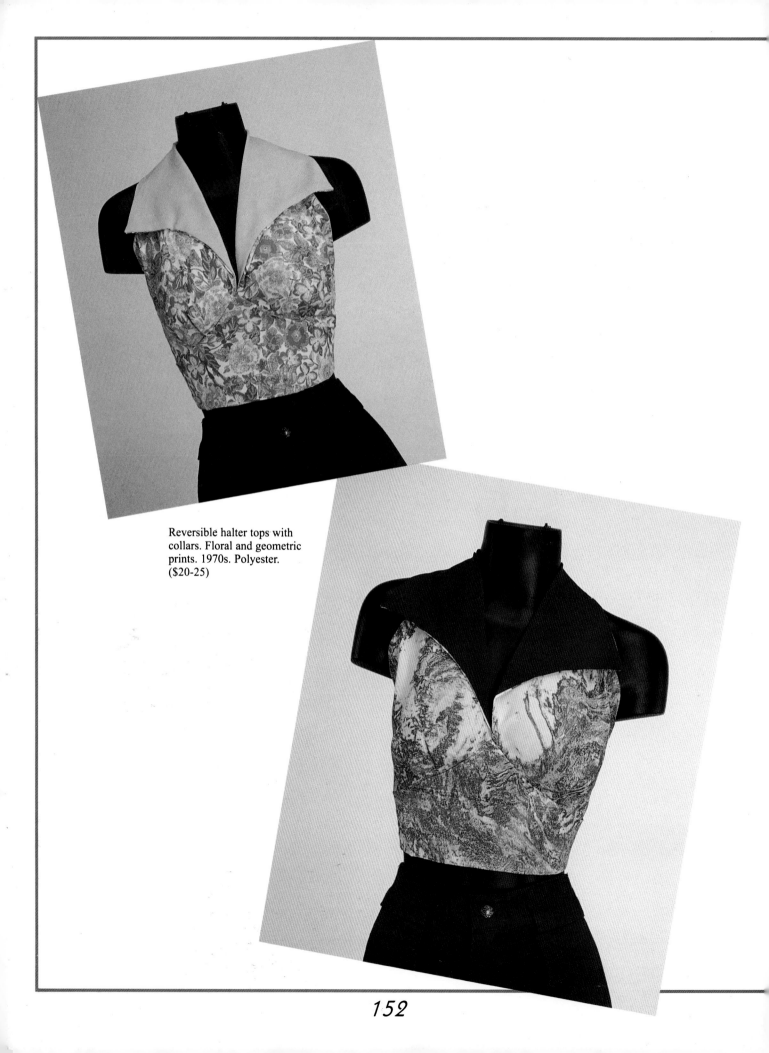

Reversible halter tops with
collars. Floral and geometric
prints. 1970s. Polyester.
($20-25)

Reversible halter tops with collars. Floral and geometric prints. 1970s. Polyester. ($20-25)

Low-cut halter top that ties at neck and back. Cartoon figures at "Happy Hour." 1970s. Stretch polyester. *Courtesy of Barbara Schuette.* ($20-25)

Model wearing high-cut halter with hip huggers.

154

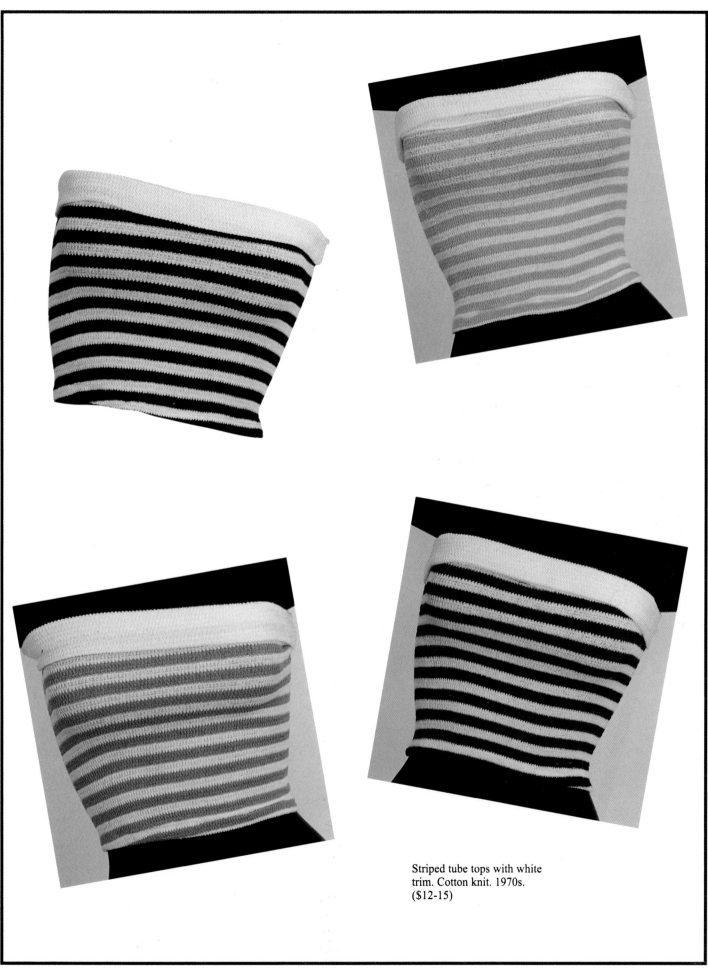

Striped tube tops with white
trim. Cotton knit. 1970s.
($12-15)

Model wearing Maverick® hot
pants with button-fly front. Blue
denim patchwork pattern. Cotton.
1970s. ($24-30)

SHORT SHORTS

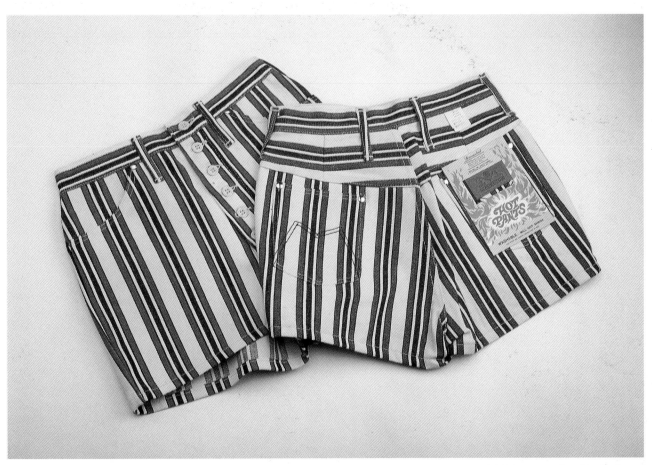

Maverick® hot pants. Double zip front.
Polyester/cotton. 1970s. ($24-30)

Maverick® hot pants with button-
fly front. Vertical stripes. 100
percent cotton. 1970s. ($24-30)

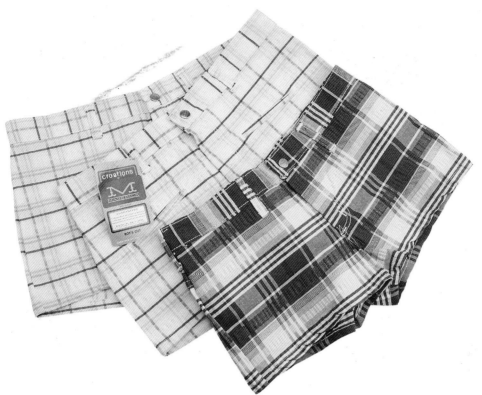

Maverick® "Boy's Cut" hot pants. Slash pockets on front. Plaid patterns. Polyester/cotton. 1970s. ($24-30)

Short Shorts

Maverick® hot pants. Red-and-blue bandanna prints. 100 percent cotton. 1970s. ($24-30)

Maverick® "Boy's cut" hot pants. Denim with patch pockets. 100 percent cotton. 1970s. ($24-30)

In The Groove

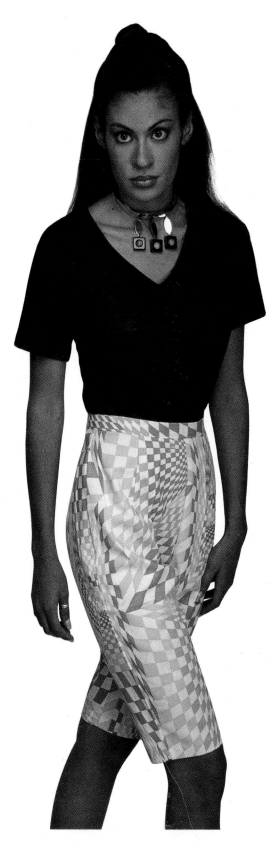